OUR FIVE OCEANS

PACIFIC OCEAN

Megan Kopp

www.av2books.com

AV² provides enriched content that supplements and complements this book. Weigl's AV² books strive to create inspired learning and engage young minds in a total learning experience.

Your AV² Media Enhanced books come alive with...

Audio
Listen to sections of the book read aloud.

Key Words
Study vocabulary, and complete a matching word activity.

Video
Watch informative video clips.

Quizzes
Test your knowledge.

Embedded Weblinks
Gain additional information for research.

Slide Show
View images and captions, and prepare a presentation.

Try This!
Complete activities and hands-on experiments.

... and much, much more!

Go to **www.av2books.com**, and enter this book's unique code.

BOOK CODE

T635829

AV² by Weigl brings you media enhanced books that support active learning.

Published by AV² by Weigl
350 5th Avenue, 59th Floor
New York, NY 10118
Website: www.av2books.com

Library of Congress Cataloging-in-Publication Data

Names: Kopp, Megan, author.
Title: Pacific Ocean / Megan Kopp.
Description: New York, NY : AV2 by Weigl, [2018] | Series: Our five oceans | Includes index.
Identifiers: LCCN 2016016453 (print) | LCCN 2016017965 (ebook) | ISBN 9781489647399 (hardcover : alk. paper) | ISBN 9781489650924 (softcover : alk. paper) | ISBN 9781489647405 (Multi-user ebk.)
Subjects: LCSH: Pacific Ocean--Juvenile literature.
Classification: LCC GC771 .K686 2017 (print) | LCC GC771 (ebook) | DDC 910.9164--dc23
LC record available at https://lccn.loc.gov/2016016453

Printed in the United States of America in Brainerd, Minnesota
1 2 3 4 5 6 7 8 9 0 20 19 18 17 16

112016
040416

Project Coordinator: Katie Gillespie

Photo Credits
Every reasonable effort has been made to trace ownership and to obtain permission to reprint copyright material. The publishers would be pleased to have any errors or omissions brought to their attention so that they may be corrected in subsequent printings.

Weigl acknowledges Getty Images, Corbis, Alamy, Shutterstock, iStock, and Dreamstime as its primary image suppliers for this title.

CONTENTS

Global Ocean

"If you think the ocean isn't important, imagine Earth without it. Mars comes to mind. No ocean, no life support system."

Sylvia Earle, Oceanographer

Earth is often called "the blue planet" because of the ocean waters that cover almost three-quarters of its surface across both **hemispheres**. About 3.8 billion years ago, the ocean began forming. Gases in the atmosphere formed clouds causing rain to fall. Some of the ocean water was originally this rain and some came from icy comets that crashed into Earth. It was in the ocean that life on Earth first began. Ocean life is varied, ranging from plants and animals too tiny to see with the unaided eye, to massive whales.

Most of the oxygen that humans breathe is produced in the ocean. The ocean also absorbs about half of all the harmful gases, such as carbon dioxide and methane, that human activities release into the atmosphere. Many people get their food from the ocean as well.

Earth has only one ocean, with many basins. Ocean basins are made up of the sea floor, and features such as islands, trenches, and ridges. The large ocean basins have been given names. The Arctic Ocean is the smallest basin in the global ocean. It is followed in size by the Southern Ocean, Indian Ocean, and Atlantic Ocean. The Pacific Ocean is the largest ocean basin on Earth.

The Pacific Ocean serves as a route for the transportation of goods and people. It provides opportunities for play and inspires creativity. The Pacific Ocean has also played a very important role in the growth of many cultures.

Light is not visible farther down than **3,280 feet** in an ocean. (1 kilometer)

Coral reefs provide places for animals such as reef octopuses to catch food or find shelter.

The average depth of the global ocean is **2.5 miles**. (4 km)

The **largest animal** that has ever lived on Earth, the blue whale, lives in the global ocean.

The Pacific Ocean

The Largest Ocean

The Pacific Ocean covers almost one third of Earth's surface. In area, the Pacific Ocean is twice the size of the Atlantic Ocean, and contains more than twice as much water. The Pacific Ocean covers about 5,900,000 square miles (15,281,000 square km). It is about 15 times the size of the United States. This massive body of water stretches from the Arctic Ocean to the Southern Ocean. The Pacific Ocean lies between Asia and Australia on the west, and North America and South America on the east. The salt content of the water varies, depending on factors including depth and recent rainfall. In the southeast, water in the Pacific Ocean averages a salty 37 Practical Salinity Units (PSUs). Near the Arctic Ocean, salt content drops to a much less salty 32 PSUs.

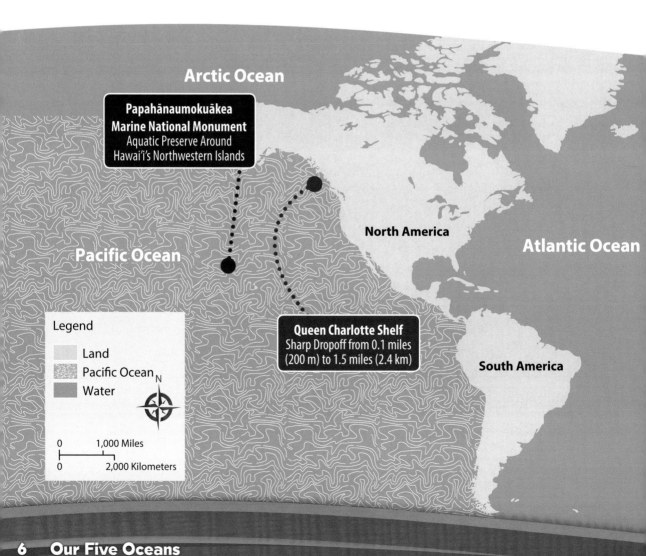

Arctic Ocean

Papahānaumokuākea Marine National Monument Aquatic Preserve Around Hawai'i's Northwestern Islands

Pacific Ocean

North America

Atlantic Ocean

Queen Charlotte Shelf Sharp Dropoff from 0.1 miles (200 m) to 1.5 miles (2.4 km)

South America

Legend

Land
Pacific Ocean
Water

N

0   1,000 Miles

0   2,000 Kilometers

The average depth of the Pacific Ocean, without adjacent smaller bodies of water, is 14,040 feet (4,280 meters), and its greatest known depth is 36,201 feet (11,034 m). The Challenger Deep is the world's deepest point. It lies in the Mariana Trench in the Pacific Ocean.

The Pacific Ocean covers more square miles (km) than all the land on Earth combined.

The Pacific Ocean is also home to many coral reefs. The largest coral reef system on Earth, the Great Barrier Reef, lies just off the coast of Queensland, Australia, in the South Pacific. The reef supports a wide range of species and is so large that it can be seen from outer space.

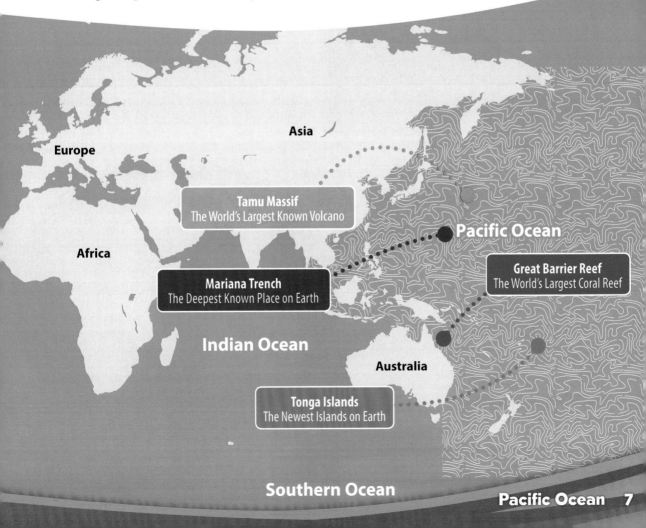

Europe

Asia

Tamu Massif
The World's Largest Known Volcano

Africa

Pacific Ocean

Mariana Trench
The Deepest Known Place on Earth

Great Barrier Reef
The World's Largest Coral Reef

Indian Ocean

Australia

Tonga Islands
The Newest Islands on Earth

Southern Ocean

Pacific Ocean Currents and Climate

The ocean regulates Earth's **climate** by absorbing heat and spreading it out around the world. Currents move heat through ocean water, and the water cycle moves heat between the ocean and the atmosphere. By absorbing some of the heat and gases that cause climate change, the ocean helps to slow down the effects of global warming.

A large mass of warm water off the coast of North America was discovered in 2013 and grew for three years before breaking up. The water was too warm for phytoplankton, which is an important food for many marine animals.

Temperature

Temperatures vary across the Pacific Ocean. Areas in its northern limits have long, cold winters and short, mild summers. Island nations in the South Pacific are temperate all year long. The Pacific Ocean's waters also vary in temperature and are shaped by the currents, which carry water of various temperatures. The deepest waters have consistent temperatures that average about 38° Fahrenheit (3° Celsius). This cold-water layer is closer to the surface along the coasts of North and Central America than it is in the central and western Pacific.

Wind

The huge stretch of open water over the Pacific Ocean affects the wind and pressure patterns over it. In the southern and eastern Pacific, trade winds are among the steadiest winds on Earth. Trade winds are winds that blow toward the equator and average about 15 miles (24 km) per hour. Violent storms have been known to occur over an area of the Pacific Ocean called the trade wind belt. Cyclones happen when particularly strong winds spiral inward.

The word *typhoon* is only used to describe severe cyclones that develop in the northwest Pacific.

Precipitation

The wide, open Pacific is a major factor in determining where and how much it rains. Along the equator, the Pacific Ocean has periods of increased wetter and drier climates every three to seven years. El Niño is a warm ocean event. It increases the odds for dry winters across the northern United States and wet winters across the south. La Niña is a cooler ocean event. It also changes normal weather patterns. La Niña's cold currents bring cold winters to North America.

The Pacific Ocean receives an average of 50 inches (127 centimeters) of rain per year.

Changing Climate

Earth's climate changes naturally over thousands of years. However, human activity over the past several hundred years has dramatically increased this rate of change. **Greenhouse gases** trap heat within Earth's atmosphere. Human activities, such as burning fossil fuels, are creating more gases than is environmentally sustainable. Climate change creates rising sea levels and warming ocean temperatures. Storms will be larger, and there will be extremes in weather, from droughts to floods. In the Pacific Ocean in particular, rising sea levels will have significant impacts on coastal industries and ecosystems.

As Pacific Ocean levels rise, the salt water from the ocean can pollute fresh water and threaten freshwater fish.

Pacific Peoples

The first people arrived at the western edge of the Pacific Ocean near Papua New Guinea at least as early as 30,000 BC. Other peoples arrived much later, blending with the ancient Papuan tribes. The Pacific Ocean separates Pacific cultures. This separation allowed for diversity between different island populations. However, the cultural significance of the ocean is recognized across many Pacific cultures.

Māori

Ancestors of today's Māori came from eastern Pacific islands in the 13th century. They discovered New Zealand through a series of voyages. These early explorers sailed using ocean currents and winds, and the stars for navigation. Small groups arrived and settled in small hunting bands. The Māori hunted seals and large, flightless birds called moa. Crops were planted and people moved inland, but birds, fish, and shellfish remained an important part of the Māori diet.

Hawai'ians

The first Hawai'ians arrived from the Marquesas Islands, French Polynesia, about 1,600 years ago. A second wave of people came from Tahiti about 1,000 years ago. Early Hawai'ians relied on the ocean for everything from transportation to food. People owned land in wedge-shaped sections from the mountaintops down to the sea. One of the four Hawai'ian gods, Kanaloa, is associated with the ocean and long-distance voyages.

Haida

Haida Gwaii is an **archipelago** off the northern coast of British Columbia, Canada. Historically, Haida lived on these islands and in southern Alaska. The Pacific Ocean was the main source of food for the people. The ocean provided salmon, halibut, seaweed, whales, clams, and animals such as seals and turtles. Fish oils were used for flavoring food and became an important trade item.

The Myth of Tangaroa

Myths are familiar stories passed on from generation to generation by word of mouth. Around the world, myths help explain mysteries, such as where people came from and how they relate to the natural world. Myths blend fact and fiction, combining magical elements with reality.

In Māori culture, the sea is considered the source and foundation of all life. Tangaroa is the god of the sea. He is one of the sons of Sky Father, Rangi, and Earth Mother, Papa. Tangaroa and his brothers separated their parents, allowing for life to flourish between the sky and Earth. Rangi missed Papa so much he cried hundreds of tears, creating the ocean. Tangaroa's brother, Tawhiri, god of wind and storms, took pity on their father. Tawhiri sent storms to punish his brothers for separating their parents. Tangaroa fled into the ocean. The fish followed their father into the ocean, but the reptiles were scared and hid in the forests. This made Tangaroa angry. It is believed that Tangaroa, in the form of the ocean, is eating away at the land in order to be reunited with his children.

Exploration and Trade

"The world's finest wilderness lies beneath the waves."
Robert Wyland, Marine Life Artist

Ancient Polynesians explored and settled many of the Pacific islands, approximately 4,000 years ago. They used the Sun, stars, and ocean currents. These all helped them to navigate and sail large voyaging canoes across the Pacific Ocean.

European exploration of the Pacific Ocean began with the Spanish and Portuguese in the early 1500s, as they searched for new territories, new wealth, and new trade partners. In the 17th century, Dutch explorers encountered inhabited islands dotting the ocean while looking for new trading routes. The British and the French explored the Pacific Ocean in the 18th century, and Captain James Cook made his first trip to the Pacific. He mapped many Pacific islands, including Tahiti and Bora-Bora.

Pacific explorers headed into the deep ocean in the 1950s and 1960s, in order to discover its depth, and attempt to identify new marine species. Advancements in technology enabled the discovery of new species of marine life near volcanic vents. In 2005, an entirely new grouping of animal life was found.

Pacific Ocean Exploration

2000 to 1000 BC People arrive in Polynesia in large sailing canoes.

1572 English explorer Francis Drake brings the first news of the Pacific Ocean's vast resources back to Europe.

500 BC   1500 AD   1600

1513 AD The first Europeans discover the eastern border of the Pacific Ocean. They are members of an expedition led by Vasco Núñez de Balboa.

1642 Dutch explorer Abel Tasman discovers New Zealand.

What's in a Name?

The Pacific Ocean was named by Portuguese explorer Ferdinand Magellan. He called this body of water *Mar Pacifico*. This means "the peaceful sea," in Italian, Spanish, and Portuguese. Magellan gave the Pacific Ocean this name after he sailed the ocean for three months without encountering any storms.

The largest ships in Europe in the 1500s were called carracks. These were the first ships to be sailed through the Pacific.

2016 Scientists work to fully map the area around the Mariana Trench.

1768 Captain James Cook searches for a fabled southern continent. He discovers the eastern coast of Australia.

2000

1700

1800

1963 Geologist J. Tuzo Wilson develops the hot spot theory, which explains how the Hawai'ian islands were formed.

Pacific Ocean Ecosystems

All **organisms** need food, water, shelter, and space in order to survive. **Producers** such as phytoplankton get their energy from the Sun. **Consumers** get energy by eating other organisms. Herbivores are consumers that eat only plants, carnivores are consumers that eat other animals, and omnivores eat both plants and animals. Decomposers eat the remains of dead plants and animals. Parasites live off other living plants or animals.

Food Web

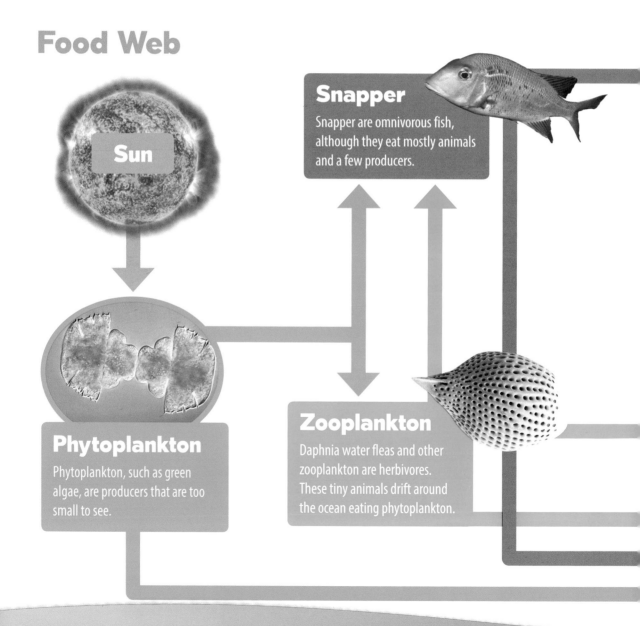

Sun

Snapper
Snapper are omnivorous fish, although they eat mostly animals and a few producers.

Phytoplankton
Phytoplankton, such as green algae, are producers that are too small to see.

Zooplankton
Daphnia water fleas and other zooplankton are herbivores. These tiny animals drift around the ocean eating phytoplankton.

This cycling of energy, as producers make energy from the Sun and consumers eat producers or each other, is called a food chain. Producers and consumers have an interdependent relationship, and the space that they live in is called an ecosystem. A food web shows how producers and consumers all need each other. If one part of the web is changed, the other parts change, too.

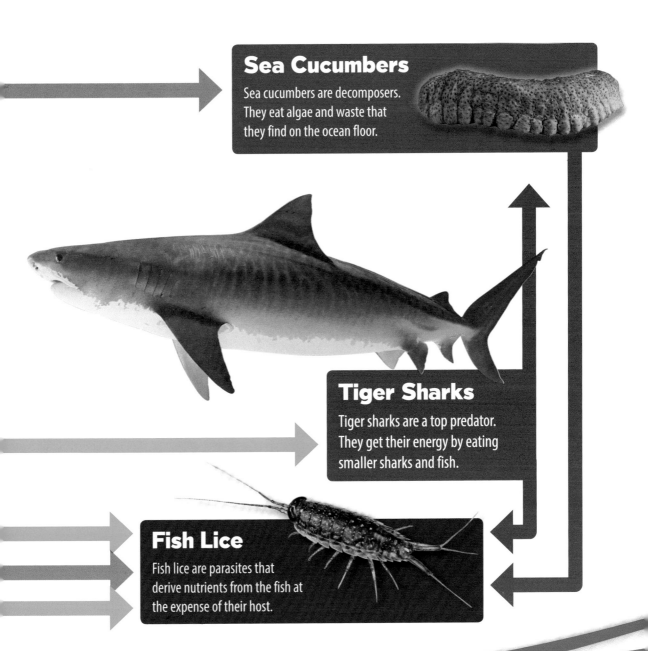

Sea Cucumbers

Sea cucumbers are decomposers. They eat algae and waste that they find on the ocean floor.

Tiger Sharks

Tiger sharks are a top predator. They get their energy by eating smaller sharks and fish.

Fish Lice

Fish lice are parasites that derive nutrients from the fish at the expense of their host.

Pacific Ocean Life

Many different species of plants and animals can be found in the Pacific Ocean. Coral reefs alone are home to millions of species. These include fish, mammals, and **invertebrates**. Organisms in the Pacific have many adaptations that make them well suited to life in this vast and varied ocean.

Gray Whales

These massive whales can reach up to 50 feet (15.3 m) in length and weigh up to 40 tons (36,300 kilograms). They migrate 12,430 miles (20,000 km) in a round trip from their feeding areas near Alaska, to their winter breeding areas off the Mexican coast, and back again. Gray whales were once hunted to near **extinction**. Today, gray whales are protected. Their population is growing, and gray whales were taken off the United States' endangered species list in 1994.

The Whale Sanctuary of El Vizcaíno, in Mexico, is recognized as an important breeding site for gray whales.

Kelp forests are a habitat in their own right and are home to hundreds of organisms.

Giant Kelp

Giant kelp is a large producer called an algae. It grows in underwater forests along the Pacific coast. Long stalks anchor each kelp to the sea floor, and they grow up to 175 feet (53 m) high. Unlike corals or most producers, kelp can grow extremely rapidly. This makes kelp forests an important source of food for many animals. Kelp forest ecosystems are home to a variety of animals, including seals, sea lions, great blue herons, and shore birds.

Sockeye Salmon

Like all Pacific salmon, sockeye are large migratory fish that are born in freshwater, but live in the ocean for up to four years. In the ocean, they feed on tiny, shrimp-like orange krill. This gives salmon meat its orange color. Adult sockeye salmon weigh as much as 15 pounds (7 kg). Sockeye salmon are the third most common species of salmon in the Pacific. While most groups of fish are referred to as schools, a group of sockeye salmon is called a bind or a run.

Sockeye salmon only turn red as they head upstream to their breeding grounds.

Sea Otters

The sea otter is a large member of the weasel family, weighing 65 pounds (30 kg) on average. Sea otters live in the northern Pacific Ocean. They spend most of their time in the water, floating on their backs to eat and sleep. Otters have thick fur that keeps them warm and dry. Sea otters were hunted close to extinction. There is now a ban on hunting sea otters. Today, their population is close to 150,000.

Sea otters open shellfish by putting a rock on their chests and hitting the rock with a shell until the shell breaks open.

Marine Iguanas

Marine iguanas can dive more than 30 feet (9 m) down into the ocean.

The marine iguana is the only species of lizard on Earth that can find food in the ocean. Marine iguanas eat underwater algae and seaweed. Marine iguanas live on the Galápagos Islands, 600 miles (965 km) off the coast of Ecuador. They range from 4 to 5 feet (1.2 to 1.4 m) in length and weigh 1 to 3 pounds (0.5 to 1.4 kg).

Pacific Life in Danger

For hundreds of years, people have looked upon the Pacific Ocean as a source of endless food and a suitable place to dispose of waste. However, both of these practices negatively affect the plants and animals that live in the Pacific Ocean. Many species of marine life are classified as vulnerable or threatened and could one day become extinct. In order to help preserve Pacific Ocean life, people must understand the challenges these plants and animals face. Research helps people learn about and begin to understand these organisms.

Write a Research Report

Learn more about why the Pacific Ocean's threatened animals matter by writing a research report. Research one of the case studies provided, or choose your own Pacific Ocean animal. Consider the animal both as an individual species, and as part of an ecosystem. Share your research with a partner and discuss your findings.

1. Choose a specific topic to research.
2. Decide what kinds of information you need to gather.
3. Research as much information as you can. Use multiple sources, such as books, magazines, online resources, newspapers, and experts on the subject.
4. Take notes about the facts you find in your research. Be sure to keep track of your sources so you can list them in a **bibliography** at the end of your report.
5. Create an outline for your report. Decide which facts should go in the introduction, body, and conclusion.
6. Use your notes to write a report in your own words. Try to explore multiple perspectives on the topic, where possible.
   - Your introduction should give a brief overview of your research topic.
   - Each body paragraph should deal with a separate subject, supporting your overall research topic.
   - The concluding paragraph should summarize the topics covered in the body of your paper.

Case Study #1

Species: Hawai'ian Monk Seal   **Status:** Critically Endangered   **Population:** 1,153

The Hawai'ian monk seal lives in the waters off the coast of a chain of islands northwest of the main Hawai'ian archipelago. It feeds on fish, spiny lobsters, octopuses, and eels. A monk seal can live up to 30 years and weigh up to 600 pounds (272 kg). Although they live in a protected habitat, Hawai'ian monk seals often become entangled in fishers' nets when they go outside of this habitat.

Case Study #2

Species: Blue Coral

Status: Near Vulnerable

Population: Unknown

Coral is made up of tiny, tube-shaped animals called polyps. Each polyp has a mouth surrounded by eight tentacles. These tiny arms help the animal capture food, such as plankton. The largest known colony of blue coral is located off the coast of Ishigaki Island in southeast Japan. Coral are vulnerable to pollution. Their skeletons are collected by people who make jewelry and ornaments.

Changing Earth

Oceans can change the land surrounding them. Some of these changes take hundreds or thousands of years, while others may take only minutes. These changes can be small, such as tides wearing away and breaking down coral or shells into sand through **erosion**. They can also be large and destructive, such as damage brought about by a typhoon or a cyclone.

Coral reef islands naturally change shape and move to new places in response to shifting **sediment**. The coral animals use this sediment to build reefs. As one side of the island is eroded, the other side grows, as sediment is deposited. Scientists have found that in a study of 600 coral reef islands, about 80 percent of the islands have remained the same or increased in size. Some islands grew by as much as 14 acres (5.6 hectares) in a single decade.

The continuous battering of waves against the coast can cause coastal erosion. Often, this results in the formation of caves.

A recent study warns that oceans will rise between **2.5 and 6.5 feet** by 2100. (0.8 and 2.0 m)

Approximately **90 percent** of all earthquakes occur around the edges of the Pacific Ocean.

Rising sea levels are also changing Earth and creating trouble for Pacific island nations. Many low-lying coral **atolls** reach less than 13 feet (4 m) above sea level. As sea levels rise and mix with existing fresh water, freshwater supplies become limited. Flooding occurs during high tides as sea water comes up through the porous coral of the atolls. It also becomes difficult to grow food crops because this sea water makes the soil too salty.

Pacific Ocean storms are becoming larger and more forceful. Wave energy typically increases by about 20 percent during an El Niño winter. Storm waves combined with high tides often reach up on cliffs and cause erosion. This is an ongoing issue along the California coast, where vanishing coastlines cause problems for people and animals.

Below the Waves

Countries bordering the Pacific Ocean often experience earthquakes and volcanic eruptions. Most active volcanoes are found along the boundaries of Earth's **tectonic plates**. The tectonic plates float or move on top of a soft, hot layer of **magma** lying below. Many volcanoes are found on the ocean floor where the tectonic plates are moving apart. One particularly active zone is a horseshoe-shaped area known as "the Ring of Fire." Multiple tectonic plates meet and form a ring. These plates push against one another, creating active volcanoes.

Underwater earthquakes sometimes cause **tsunamis**. As these waves travel across the water toward land, they become larger. Tsunamis can travel as fast as 500 miles (800 km) per hour in deep ocean water, but they slow down as the ocean depth decreases. Although they were once known as tidal waves, tsunamis are not caused by tides.

Coral reefs grow as much as **4 feet** each year. (1.2 m)

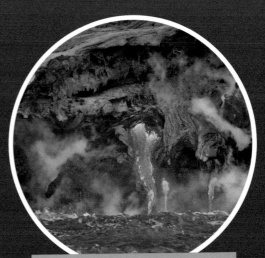

Kilauea on the Big Island, Hawai'i, began erupting in January 1983, and has been erupting continuously ever since.

Pacific Ocean Uses

The Pacific Ocean has provided people with food, resources, and transportation routes for thousands of years. It has facilitated some of the most exciting explorations. The Pacific provides a low-cost sea transportation route between east and west.

Salmon fishing is a major industry off North America. Herring, bonito, and shrimp are harvested in Japanese and Russian fisheries. The anchovy harvest is important off the coast of Peru. Seaweed is a key Pacific Ocean food resource for Japan and Korea.

Underwater drilling for oil has been done in the Pacific Ocean off the coasts of California and China, and a few minerals have been mined. Rare-earth elements are used to make parts for electronics. Some deep-ocean mud has high concentrations of these elements. It is estimated that an area of only 0.4 square miles (1 sq. km) could provide one-fifth of the current demand for these elements.

The Pacific Ocean also draws people from around the world, for its natural beauty, and for the plants and animals that live there. The tourism industry creates many jobs in Pacific island countries. Tourism, in particular ecotourism, is the main economic activity in the Galápagos Islands. Ecotourism is a form of tourism where people travel to see the unique plants and animals of the Pacific Ocean without damaging their environment. People must maintain a fine balance between enjoying ecotourism and managing the visitors' impact on a fragile ecosystem.

Fishways are pathways created to allow salmon to pass through human structures that would otherwise be barriers to salmon migration.

Each year, more than **750,000 pounds** of pearls are harvested from the Pacific Ocean. (340,000 kg)

More than **90 percent** of Americans take part in water-based tourism each year.

In 2015, the total allowable catch for snow crab in the Bering Sea was **40.6 million pounds**. (18.4 million kg)

Where Do You Stand?

The floor of the Pacific Ocean holds vast amounts of natural resources, such as copper, nickel, and gold. New technology has now made it possible for companies to mine the seabed. The world's first deep-sea mining project will begin in the waters around Papua New Guinea in 2018. Consider the following perspectives. With whom do you agree and why?

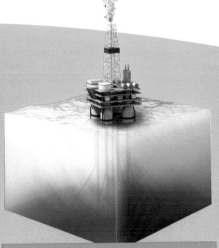

People already extract large quantities of oil from the seabed. Sometimes, there are high environmental costs.

Deep-Sea Mining

For	Against
Mining Companies "Impacts and discharges from sea floor mining will all occur on the deep sea floor without exposing coastal coral reefs or fisheries to any contaminants."	**Environmental Organizations** "Deep-sea mining will result in direct and indirect impacts. Each mining job will directly destroy thousands of amazing vent formations and their irreplaceable ecosystems."
Regional Governments "The deep-sea minerals industry has the potential to provide much-needed economic growth and development for the Pacific region."	**Community Members** "We need to apply the rule of care. The questions far outweigh the benefits, and it is not good for the country at this time."

Issues

The Pacific Ocean was once thought to have endless resources. People thought the ocean was unlikely to be damaged. However, human activities cause pollution, which is a major problem. Overfishing is greatly lowering the population of some fish species.

Overfishing

Overfishing occurs when more fish are caught than can be naturally replaced. Overfishing affects the ecosystem as well as the people who rely on fishing for their income. More than 85 percent of the world's fisheries are either at or beyond their ability to maintain a balance. Due to overfishing, the Pacific bluefin tuna population is down to 4 percent of its normal levels.

Pollution

The Great Pacific Garbage Patch is a popular name for marine debris that has gathered in the north Pacific Ocean. The largest collection of garbage in the Pacific is the size of Texas. Here, there is an estimated 13 pounds (6 kg) of plastic for every 2.2 pounds (1 kg) of natural plankton. However, this is not the only patch of garbage in the Pacific. Much of this garbage is so small that it cannot be seen without looking carefully. Marine debris is a growing hazard for wildlife. Animals can get caught in plastic wrapping, choke on inedible trash, or even be poisoned by chemicals found in the plastic. When marine wildlife such as fish ingest these chemicals, they become toxic to some degree. Humans then consume some of these toxic fish. The pollution of the ocean directly affects humans, as well as marine wildlife.

Acidification

Carbon dioxide is a gas that is emitted when fossil fuels are burned. It is one of the greenhouse gases that warms Earth's climate. Each year, oceans absorb almost one-quarter of all the carbon dioxide emitted. Although this may sound positive at first, it is changing acid levels in the ocean. The increasingly acidic water dissolves the protective shells of many marine species.

Protective Laws

The United Nations Convention on Biological Diversity has a target of protecting 10 percent of the world's oceans by 2020. In 2014, only 3.4 percent of the global ocean was protected from human activities, such as shipping and fishing. Most of this protection is from nations that border the ocean. Areas outside of national borders are regarded as the high seas. Any country or state is free to fish, lay pipelines, and construct artificial islands, among other activities within the high seas. Less than one-quarter of 1 percent of this area is protected.

Coral Bleaching

When corals are stressed by changes in their environment, they lose the algae living in their tissues. This makes them turn white. White coral is not dead, but it is more likely to die. Warming oceans are stressing many of the Pacific Ocean's coral reefs. Coral reefs support more species than any other marine environment. It is estimated that 19 percent of all coral reefs are going to be destroyed soon, and another 15 percent may die within 10 to 20 years.

Protecting the Pacific Ocean

The Pacific Ocean and its wildlife face serious challenges. Thankfully, countries and organizations around the world are taking action. Everyone, from ordinary citizens to scientists, can help protect the Pacific Ocean.

Institute for Ocean Conservation Science

The Institute for Ocean Conservation Science has a mission of encouraging ocean protection through scientific learning. These research projects increase human knowledge about threats to oceans and the marine life they support. The research helps build a foundation for the creation of policies to help in ocean protection. The institute is also doing research into sharks, whose populations are declining because of destructive commercial fishing practices. This research has led the United States to ban the sale of non-farmed beluga **caviar**.

Many shark species are endangered because of destructive fishing practices.

Limestone arches were formed before sea levels rose as high as current levels. The NOAA tracks these rising sea levels.

National Oceanic and Atmospheric Administration

The goal of the National Oceanic and Atmospheric Administration (NOAA) is to understand and predict changes in climate, weather, oceans, and coasts. It has provided useful information about the weather and the ocean to sailors and scientists for many years. Currently, the NOAA's research is leading efforts to uncover exactly how El Niño affects weather.

Ocean Futures Society

Jean-Michel Cousteau is the grandson of pioneer oceanographer Jacques Cousteau. Jean-Michel's Ocean Futures Society was formed to explore the global ocean, and to inspire and educate people to act responsibly for its protection. Much of the society's work is done through expeditions and documentaries. One of its films highlighted the first attempt to rehabilitate a captive orca named Keiko. The Ocean Futures Society documented the challenges of returning Keiko to freedom.

The Ocean Futures Society creates educational programs that help to raise awareness about oceans.

In 2015, Ocean Conservancy volunteers picked up 16 million pounds (7 million kg) of trash.

Ocean Conservancy

Ocean Conservancy works to create science-based solutions for a healthy ocean, and for the wildlife and communities that depend on it. It acts as a voice for the ocean. Ocean Conservancy motivates volunteer citizens to create change and protect the ocean for future generations. The organization supports research and monitoring efforts that will lead to innovative, sustainable solutions. Ocean Conservancy's International Coastal Cleanup is the world's largest volunteer effort to clean up waterways and the ocean.

Looking to the Future

"All of us have the same percentage of salt in our blood that exists in the ocean ... We are tied to the ocean."
Former U.S. President John F. Kennedy

The Pacific Ocean is changing and getting warmer. Its sea level is rising and its marine life is being altered. Some of these changes will soon be irreversible.

For 22 Pacific island countries and territories, change is inevitable. The effects of pollution, overuse, and increasing acid levels are affecting the ocean on which these nations rely for survival. The main sources of marine pollution are sewage, agricultural and manufacturing runoff, and plastic waste. According to studies, fish in the North Pacific region eat 12,000 to 24,000 tons (11,000 to 22,000 tonnes) of plastic each year.

Elephant seals were overhunted and almost driven to extinction. Populations have recovered after laws were made to protect the seals.

Many islands in the Pacific Ocean are threatened by rising sea levels.

Climate change is affecting the health of many coral reefs surrounding the Pacific islands. Reefs help protect the islands from slowly being eaten away by the waves. They are important homes for many species of marine life. A warming climate will also see more intense wind effects as El Niño events strengthen. Flooding will occur in the southeastern Pacific.

A more positive outlook depends on reliable science. Rules must be put into place to help reduce pollution and to limit overuse of the fisheries. People will need to learn to work together and to find new ways to solve the problems that the future may bring if changes are not made.

Celebrating the Oceans

The Aloha Festivals, in Hawai'i, celebrate brave and inspiring canoe builders, voyagers, and navigators. In 2013, the festivals celebrated the 40th anniversary of the Polynesian Voyaging Society, which has encouraged generations of voyagers to retrace the paths of Hawai'i's Pacific Islander ancestors. The festival also helped revive the *wa'a kaulua*, or double-hulled sailing canoe, and traditional ways of navigating, such as using the Sun and stars, and by reading wave patterns and other natural signs.

Double-hulled sailing canoes provide stability, allowing the voyagers to travel greater distances.

Quiz

1 When did Captain Cook first discover the eastern coast of Australia?

2 What happens to corals when they are stressed by changes in their environment?

3 About how many times the size of the United States is the Pacific Ocean?

4 How many Pacific island countries or territories are in danger due to pollution and rising sea levels?

5 Which country in the Pacific will see underwater mining by 2018?

6 Who named the Pacific Ocean *Mar Pacifico*?

7 What percentage of the global ocean was protected from human activities in 2014?

8 How much will oceans rise by 2100?

9 Where is Haida Gwaii?

10 How much of the world's ocean does the United Nations Convention on Biological Diversity hope to protect by 2020?

Key Words

archipelago: a group of islands

atolls: islands made of coral

bibliography: an appendix that lists the works referenced in a book or article

caviar: pickled eggs of a large fish

climate: the weather conditions in an area over a long period of time

consumers: animals that feed on plants or other animals

erosion: the gradual destruction of something by natural forces such as water, wind, or ice

extinction: the state or situation that results when something such as a plant or animal species has died out completely

greenhouse gases: gases that pollute the air and cause the warming of Earth's atmosphere

hemispheres: half of Earth, normally divided into north and south

invertebrates: animals that do not have a backbone

magma: hot fluid beneath Earth's crust

organisms: individual living things such as each individual plant or animal

producers: plants and plantlike animals that make their own food

sediment: pieces of rock, soil, and shells, moved by water and wind, that eventually settle in layers

tectonic plates: sections of Earth's crust

tsunamis: unusually large, destructive ocean waves caused by underwater earthquakes, volcanic eruptions, or coastal landslides

Index

Log on to www.av2books.com

AV² by Weigl brings you media enhanced books that support active learning. Go to www.av2books.com, and enter the special code found on page 2 of this book. You will gain access to enriched and enhanced content that supplements and complements this book. Content includes video, audio, weblinks, quizzes, a slide show, and activities.

AV² Online Navigation

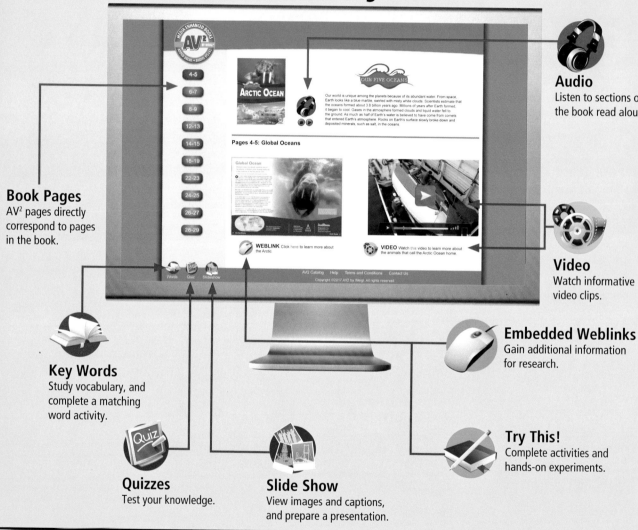

Audio
Listen to sections o
the book read alou

Book Pages
AV² pages directly correspond to pages in the book.

Video
Watch informative video clips.

Key Words
Study vocabulary, and complete a matching word activity.

Embedded Weblinks
Gain additional information for research.

Quizzes
Test your knowledge.

Slide Show
View images and captions, and prepare a presentation.

Try This!
Complete activities and hands-on experiments.

AV² was built to bridge the gap between print and digital. We encourage you to tell us what you like and what you want to see in the future.

Sign up to be an AV² Ambassador at www.av2books.com/ambassador.

Due to the dynamic nature of the Internet, some of the URLs and activities provided as part of AV² by Weigl may have changed or ceased to exist. AV² by Weigl accepts no responsibility for any such changes. All media enhanced books are regularly monitored to update addresses and sites in a timely manner. Contact AV² by Weigl at 1-866-649-3445 or av2books@weigl.com with any questions, comments, or feedback.